TELL THE T

BY ABBY BADACH

THE TALE OF
ROBIN HOOD

Please visit our website, www.enslow.com. For a free color catalog of all our high-quality books, call toll free 1-800-398-2504 or fax 1-877-980-4454.

Cataloging-in-Publication Data

Names: Doyle, Abby Badach.
Title: The tale of Robin Hood / Abby Badach Doyle.
Description: New York : Enslow Publishing, 2024. | Series: Tell the tale | Includes glossary and index.
Identifiers: ISBN 9781978535459 (pbk.) | ISBN 9781978535466 (library bound) | ISBN 9781978535473 (ebook)
Subjects: LCSH: Robin Hood (Legendary character)–Juvenile literature. | Robin Hood (Legend)–Juvenile literature. | Civilization, Medieval–Juvenile literature. | England–Civilization–1066-1485–Juvenile literature.
Classification: LCC PR2129.D69 2024 | DDC 398.22'0941–dc23

Portions of this work were originally authored by Julia McDonnell and published as *The Legend of Robin Hood*. All new material in this edition is authored by Abby Badach Doyle.

Published in 2024 by
Enslow Publishing
2544 Clinton Street
Buffalo, NY 14224

Designer: Tanya Dellaccio and Claire Wrazin
Editor: Abby Badach Doyle

Photo credits: Series Art (leather background) Rawpixel.com/Shutterstock.com, (paper background) Daboost/Shutterstock.com, (metal plate) maxstockphoto/Shutterstock.com, (explore more background) Didecs/Shutterstock.com; cover, p. 1 (Robin Hood) NGvozdeva/Shutterstock.com; cover, p. 1 (background) Midorie/Shutterstock.com; pp. 5, 21, 25 duncan1890/iStock; p. 7 (illustrations) Arthur Balitskii/Shutterstock.com; p. 9 ilbusca/iStock; p. 11 File:Woodcut_of_Robin_Hood_meeting_with_the_Maid_Marion_and_the_Sheriff_of_Nottingham.tif/Wikimedia Commons; p. 13 File:Robin Hood and Little John.jpg/Wikimedia Commons; p. 15 File:The_Merry_Adventures_of_Robin_Hood,_2_Frontispiece.png/ Wikimedia Commons; p. 17 (map) AKaiser/Shutterstock.com; p. 19 File:Josep_Juliana_Albert_La_Macelleria_1874.jpg/Wikimedia Commons; p. 22 File:Richard_coeur_de_lion.jpg/Wikimedia Commons; p. 23 File:British_Library_digitised_image_from_page_275_of_"Robin_Hood_and_ Little_John_or,_the_Merry_Men_of_Sherwood_Forest"_(11033912023).jpg/Wikimedia Commons; p. 27 Allstar Picture Library Limited/Alamy Stock Photo; p. 29 Edwin Butter/Shutterstock.com

CPSIA compliance information: Batch #CSENS24: For further information contact Enslow Publishing at 1-800-398-2504.

Find us on

CONTENTS

Words in the glossary appear in **bold** type the first time they are used in the text.

GOOD OR BAD?

Robin Hood is a hero . . . and a thief! He steals from the rich and gives to the poor. Robin Hood is one of the most well-known outlaws. An outlaw is a person who has broken the law and is hiding or running from **punishment**.

People have been telling Robin Hood's story for more than 700 years. Most people agree he wasn't a real person. Even so, his story has bits of truth. The tale of Robin Hood can teach us a lot about the history of that time.

EXPLORE MORE!

The first tales of Robin Hood were told through ballads. A ballad is a poem or song that tells a story. In the 1400s, most common people couldn't read or write. They used ballads to pass along facts and knowledge.

The **legend** of Robin Hood takes place long ago in England.

A HERO FOR THE POOR

The story of Robin Hood is set in the Middle Ages. This was a period in European history from about 500 to 1500 CE. Robin Hood was said to have lived in England as early as the 1300s.

During this time, nobles made money from common people who lived and worked on their land. Most people worked hard but made little money. The rich got richer, and the poor stayed poor. Common people felt like they had no power to change their lives. Then came the story of Robin Hood. He was a hero for the common people!

EXPLORE MORE!

In the Middle Ages, common people were called peasants. Peasants raised animals and crops. They made what they needed by hand. Serfs were a type of peasant but had a life more like enslaved people. They worked for the lords who owned the land.

MIDDLE AGES SOCIETY

king &
queen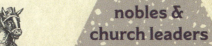

nobles &
church leaders

knights

common people

The few people at the top of society held
most of the money and power.

THE MERRY MEN

Sherwood Forest is a real place in Nottingham, England. It was used as a royal hunting ground. In the stories, Robin's crew camps and hides in Sherwood Forest. They are called the Merry Men. They hunt the king's deer that live in the forest. Some stories say the outlaws had a small group. Other stories say there were hundreds of Merry Men!

To get money, Robin and the Merry Men rob rich people who travel through the forest. However, the outlaws share their riches with anyone who needs them. They never hurt women or children.

EXPLORE MORE!

A person who hunts with a bow and arrow is called an archer. Robin Hood was very talented with his bow and arrow. He and the Merry Men practiced archery skills in the woods.

Sherwood Forest offered many places to hide.

LIFE OUTSIDE THE LAW

Robin Hood breaks the rules, but only when he feels they aren't fair. Different tales have been told about how he first became an outlaw. One story says some of the king's men tease young Robin. They say he does not have good archery skills. Then Robin shoots a deer that is very far away.

The king's men get angry. They put Robin's life in danger. Robin shoots at them for his own safety. Some stories say Robin kills one or all of them. After that, he becomes an outlaw.

EXPLORE MORE!

Robin Hood's main enemy is the sheriff of Nottingham. In the Middle Ages, a sheriff was a local government leader. The sheriff tries many different things to catch Robin. He even plays tricks on him. But Robin is always smarter and faster!

Robin disliked the sheriff but was faithful to King Richard.

ROBIN'S BEST FRIEND

Robin Hood meets his best friend, called Little John, during a fight. One day, Robin is trying to cross a log bridge. A large man wants to get across from the other side. The bridge is narrow, so there isn't room for both of them. So, Robin dares the stranger to a fight. They battle hard. Then the stranger knocks Robin into the water!

The stranger is strong, but he is also kind. Robin Hood invites him to join the Merry Men. Robin Hood and Little John become best friends.

EXPLORE MORE!

Little John and Robin Hood fought each other using long wooden poles. These were known as quarterstaves. "Stave" is another word for a big stick.

Many stories say Little John was 7 feet (2.1m) tall!

A MAN OF FAITH

A holy man named Friar Tuck serves as Robin's moral teacher. Friar Tuck is faithful to the church, but he likes to go on adventures too! Friar Tuck also lives in Sherwood Forest. Like Robin, he is strong and a skilled archer.

When they first meet, Robin asks Tuck to carry him across a stream. But Tuck refuses to carry him back. A fight begins. Then Tuck drops Robin in the water! Robin sees Tuck's strength and calls off the fight. He asks Tuck to join the Merry Men.

EXPLORE MORE!

In the Middle Ages, church was at the center of everyday life. In England, most people were Christians—people who follow the teachings of Jesus Christ. Friars were Christian teachers. They traveled among common people to pray and help the sick.

The word "friar" means "brother."

HELPING A KNIGHT

One day, the Merry Men try to rob a knight who is passing through Sherwood Forest. The knight, Sir Richard, has a sad story. He owes money to a greedy, rich man. If the knight can't pay, the man will take his land.

To help, Robin lends Sir Richard the money. Then Sir Richard visits the greedy man. He pretends to need more time to pay his **debt**. The rich man refuses. He wants that land! Then Sir Richard surprises him. He pays the money and gets to keep his land.

EXPLORE MORE!

Robin Hood is clever and kind. He knows Sir Richard is an honest man. Robin wants to help him shame the rich man for being so greedy. He doesn't want to take money from someone who has fallen on hard times.

WHERE IS SHERWOOD FOREST?

Sherwood Forest

England

Wales

A major road for travel ran through Sherwood Forest.

A TRICK AT THE MARKET

Sometimes, Robin Hood wears a **disguise** to play tricks. One day, he dresses as a butcher. Robin goes to the market and sells meat at very low prices. He gives it away for free to the poor.

The other butchers are curious. They haven't seen him at the market before. They invite him to dinner. The sheriff is there, but he doesn't recognize Robin. Robin tricks the sheriff and pretends he has cattle to sell. He leads him to the forest, where they meet the Merry Men. Then they take the sheriff's money!

EXPLORE MORE!

*Robin Hood and the Merry Men have a **polite** way of robbing people. They find rich travelers and invite them to a feast. They enjoy fine food and drink together. Afterward, they require the guest to pay a large sum.*

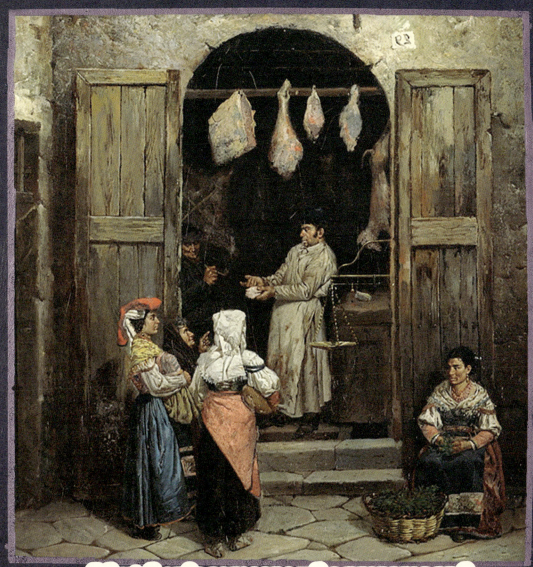

A butcher is someone who prepares and sells meat.

THE GOLDEN ARROW

In Robin Hood's time, archery is a popular sport. The sheriff holds an archery contest. He hopes Robin Hood will enter. He does . . . but in disguise! One archer hits the **target's** bull's-eye. Robin wins by splitting that arrow in half with his own.

The sheriff presents the disguised Robin with a golden arrow. Later, Robin wants to let the sheriff know he's been tricked. So, he shoots the golden arrow through the sheriff's window. It has a note stuck to it saying Robin was the real winner.

EXPLORE MORE!

*The longbow was a common **weapon** during the Middle Ages. Some longbows were taller than a grown man! Arrows shot from a longbow could travel great distances.*

It took great skill and strength to shoot a
medieval longbow.

A CLEVER STRANGER

Robin Hood is known for fooling other people. In one famous story, someone fools him! King Richard has heard stories of Robin Hood's bravery and kindness. He wonders what Robin is really like. He wants to meet him.

The king and his men disguise themselves as monks. Then they ride through Sherwood Forest, where the Merry Men stop them. They invite the monks to a feast and an archery contest. When Robin misses the target, the guests can strike him. One monk hits Robin so hard he falls to the ground!

EXPLORE MORE!

King Richard was a real person. He ruled England from 1189 to 1199 CE. He fought in wars and was brave in battle. Tales of his bravery led to his nickname, Richard the Lionheart. While he was at war, his brother Prince John ruled.

A monk is a holy man who wears a
long robe.

FREEDOM!

Whoever knocked Robin down must be very strong. The visitor pulls off his cloak to show who he truly is. It is the king! The Merry Men bow down to show their respect. They are faithful to King Richard, even though they steal and live as outlaws. They only break the rules to give back to the poor.

King Richard offers everyone **pardons**. He tells them that the news of their good deeds for the poor has spread far and wide. Robin no longer has to hide from the sheriff.

EXPLORE MORE!

The king offers Robin Hood and the Merry Men jobs as royal archers. Some stories say they live happily ever after in service of the king. Other stories say Robin Hood gets bored following the rules. He later returns to life as an outlaw.

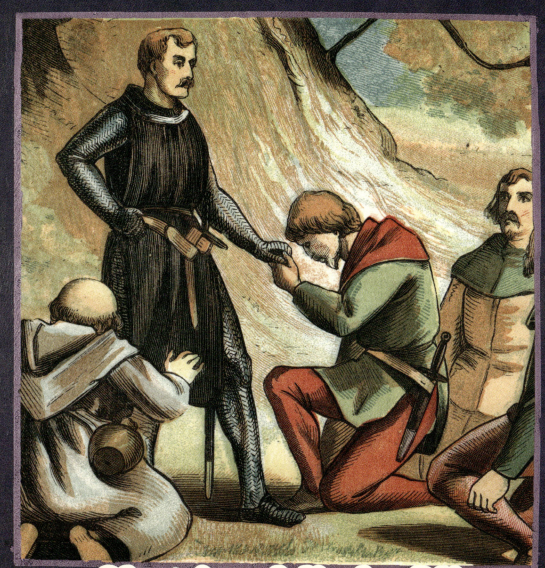

Other stories say the king shows Robin who he is during dinner.

CHANGES AND ADDITIONS

The earliest Robin Hood ballad was written down in the year 1450 CE. Before then, people told the story through poems and songs. Some pieces of the Robin Hood legend have been dropped in modern stories. The early ballads had unpleasant parts such as crimes and more deaths.

Other pieces have been added over the years. Robin Hood's love interest, Maid Marian, was not mentioned in the original ballads. Today, many movies and TV shows have been made about Robin Hood. The first of many was a silent film that came out in 1922.

EXPLORE MORE!

*Robin Hood and his men wear the color "Lincoln green." This is a dark color that helps them **blend in** with the trees of Sherwood Forest. The name comes from the city of Lincoln, England. Wool was made and dyed there.*

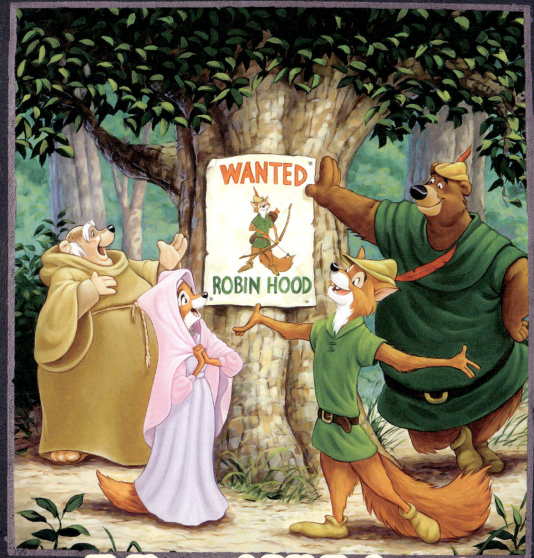

The Disney movie *Robin Hood* came out in 1973.

WAS ROBIN HOOD REAL?

Some tales say Robin Hood was a common man. Others say he was of noble birth, or even a knight. Robin Hood probably wasn't one real person who lived in history. It would be impossible for one man to be everything the stories say is true!

It's more likely that the Robin Hood legend came from the stories of many outlaws. The main truth in the Robin Hood legend is how it makes people feel. Robin Hood stands for fairness, friendship, and freedom. Those values stand the test of time!

EXPLORE MORE!

Robin is short for the name Robert. People who study history have found many records of people named Robin Hood in the Middle Ages. Sometimes the name is spelled in a different way, such as Robehod or Rabunhod.

The Major Oak, Robin's hiding place, is a real tree in Sherwood Forest.

GLOSSARY

blend in: To look like what is around you.

debt: An amount of money owed.

disguise: The state of having a false appearance.

legend: A story that has been passed down for many, many years that's unlikely to be true.

medieval: Having to do with the Middle Ages.

pardon: Forgiveness of a crime.

polite: Good mannered.

punishment: Something that is done to make someone hurt in some way for doing something wrong.

robe: A long, loose piece of clothing.

target: A round board with circles on it that you try to hit with arrows.

weapon: Something used to fight an enemy.

FOR MORE INFORMATION

BOOKS

Harper, Benjamin. *Robin Hood, Time Traveler: A Graphic Novel.* Mankato, MN: Capstone Press, 2020.

Pyle, Howard. *The Adventures of Robin Hood.* Edited by John Burrows. New York, NY: Union Square Kids, 2022.

Pyle, Howard. *The Merry Adventures of Robin Hood.* New York, NY: Union Square Kids, 2023.

WEBSITES

Britannica Kids: Robin Hood
kids.britannica.com/students/article/Robin-Hood/276750
Learn how the Robin Hood legend fits into history and how the tale has been told over time.

HGTV: Make a Robin Hood Kid's Costume for Halloween
hgtv.com/design/make-and-celebrate/handmade/kids-halloween-costume-robin-hood
Ask a trusted adult for help with this fun sewing project.

LearnEnglish Kids: Robin Hood
learnenglishkids.britishcouncil.org/listen-and-watch/short-stories/robin-hood
Read the Robin Hood story and watch a video.

INDEX